Thank you for your pu

Hello Coloring Enthusiast!

I'm thrilled you chose my coloring book for your artistic journey. These bold and simple designs were indeed crafted with alcohol markers in mind — designed to let your creativity flow with vibrant colors!

To ensure the best coloring experience, here's a friendly heads-up: alcohol markers, while fantastic for blending and vivid hues, can sometimes be a bit naughty with bleed-through. Fear not! I've got your back.

Consider placing a thin piece of cardstock between pages before diving into your masterpiece. This simple trick will keep the colors vibrant on the current page without accidentally tagging the next one. Voilà! Your coloring adventure just got even more enjoyable.

Your positive experience means the world to me, and if you could spare a moment, a glowing review would be greatly appreciated. Your support as one creative to another fuels my small business and helps it blossom. Let's color our way to a brighter, more vibrant world together!

Thank you for choosing my coloring book to bring your imagination to life. Happy coloring, and may your creations be as vibrant as your spirit!

Cheers to colorful moments,

Brooke Nolan

please share your completed work with @brooke.nolan_ #bibicreates

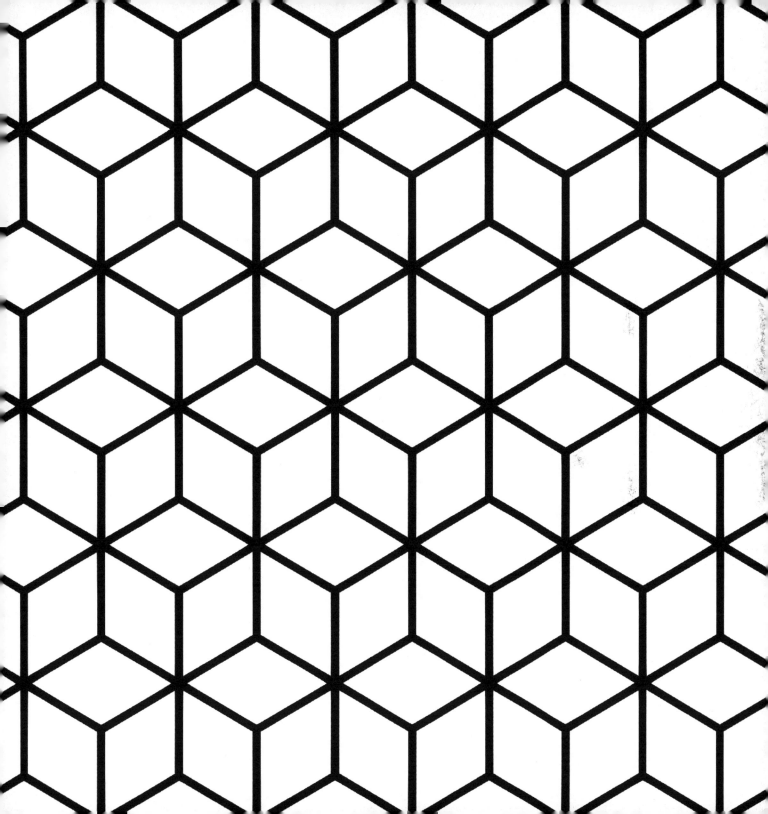

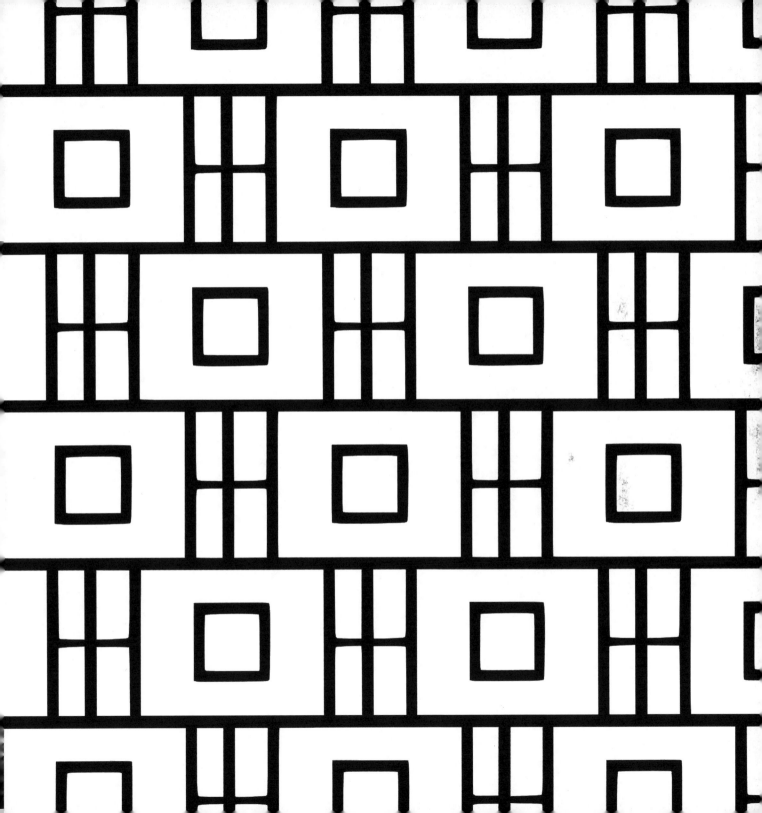

Made in the USA
Columbia, SC
27 November 2024

47737164R00059